Bees

Debbie and Brendan Gallagher

Marshall Cavendish
Benchmark

New York

Other Marshall Cavendish Offices:
Marshall Cavendish Ltd. 5th Floor, 32-38 Saffron Hill, London EC1N 8 FH, UK • Marshall Cavendish International (Asia) Private Limited, 1 New Industrial Road, Singapore 536196 • Marshall Cavendish International (Thailand) Co Ltd. 253 Asoke, 12th Flr, Sukhumvit 21 Road, Klongtoey Nua, Wattana, Bangkok 10110, Thailand • Marshall Cavendish (Malaysia) Sdn Bhd, Times Subang, Lot 46, Subang Hi-Tech Industrial Park, Batu Tiga, 40000 Shah Alam, Selangor Darul Ehsan, Malaysia

Marshall Cavendish is a trademark of Times Publishing Limited

All websites were available and accurate when this book was sent to press.

Library of Congress Cataloging-in-Publication Data

Gallagher, Debbie, 1969–
  Bees / Debbie Gallagher.
    p. cm. — (Mighty minibeasts)
  Includes index.
  Summary: "Discusses the features, habitat, food, life cycle, living habits, and unique behaviors of bees"—Provided by publisher.
  ISBN 978-1-60870-543-6
  1. Bees—Juvenile literature. I. Title.
  QL568.A6 G35 2012
  595.79/9—dc22

                                    9781608705436

First published in 2011 by
MACMILLAN EDUCATION AUSTRALIA PTY LTD
15–19 Claremont Street, South Yarra 3141

Visit our website at www.macmillan.com.au or go directly to www.macmillanlibrary.com.au

Associated companies and representatives throughout the world.

Copyright Text © Debbie Gallagher 2011

Publisher: Carmel Heron
Commissioning Editor: Niki Horin
Managing Editor: Vanessa Lanaway
Editor: Tim Clarke
Proofreader: Gill Owens
Designer: Kerri Wilson (cover and text)
Page layout: Domenic Lauricella
Photo researcher: Debbie Gallagher
Illustrator: Gaston Vanzet
Production Controller: Vanessa Johnson

Printed in China

Acknowledgments
The authors and the publisher are grateful to the following for permission to reproduce copyright material:

Front cover photograph: A bee collecting nectar © B.G. Thomson.
Photographs courtesy of: ANTPhoto.com.au/N.H.P.A., 15 (bottom); Auscape/Atsuo Fujimaru-Nature Production, 16; Stephen Buchmann, 9 (bottom); Bugwood.org, photo by Joseph Berger, 10 (bottom); Corbis/Gallo Images, 4, 11 (bottom left); Getty Images/Steve Hopkin, 8 (left), /Christian Senger, 12; iStockphoto/Nathan McClunie, 8 (top right); Minden Pictures/ Cyril Ruoso, 24; PDPhoto.org, 20 (center); Photolibrary/Alamy/ blickwinkel, 30, /Carson Baldwin Jr, 20, /Anthony Bannister, 20 (top), /Scott Camazine, 15 (top), /Fotosearch Value, 22, /Otto Hahn, 11 (top left), /Satoshi Kuribayashi, 7, 9 (top), 11 (top right), 19, /Nature Picture Library, 21 (bottom), /Hans Pfletschinger, 14 (top), /Photo Researchers, 26, /James H Robinson, 21 (bottom), /Horst Sollinger, 14 (bottom), /SPL/Nuridsany & Perennou, 27, /Leen Van Der Slik, 25; Shutterstock/LilKar, 17, /Monkey Business Images, 29, /Christian Musat, 13, /M Pace, 20 (bottom), /Vladimir Sazonov, 10 (top), /Alex Staroseltsev, 23, /Nikita Tiunov, 3, 5; B.G. Thomson, 1, 6, 11 (bottom right); USDA/Jack Dykinga, 8 (bottom right).

While every care has been taken to trace and acknowledge copyright, the publisher tenders their apologies for any accidental infringement where copyright has proved untraceable. They would be pleased to come to a suitable arrangement with the rightful owner in each case.

1 3 5 6 4 2

Contents

When a word is printed in **bold**, you can look up its meaning in the Glossary on page 31.

Mighty Minibeasts

Minibeasts are small animals, such as flies and spiders. Although they are small, minibeasts are a mighty collection of animals. They belong to three animal groups: arthropods, molluscs, or annelids.

	Animal Group		
	Arthropods	**Molluscs**	**Annelids**
Main Feature	Arthropods have an outer skeleton and a body that is divided into sections.	Most molluscs have a soft body that is not divided into sections.	Annelids have a soft body made up of many sections.
Examples of Minibeasts	Insects, such as ants, beetles, cockroaches, and wasps **Arachnids**, such as spiders and scorpions Centipedes and millipedes	Snails and slugs	Earthworms Leeches

More than three-quarters of all animals are minibeasts!

Bees

Bees are minibeasts. They belong to the arthropod group of animals. This means they have an outer skeleton and a body divided into sections. Bees are a type of insect.

Bees are closely related to ants and wasps.

What Do Bees Look Like?

Bees have a body that is divided into three main parts. These parts are the head, the **thorax**, and the **abdomen**. They have four wings and six legs.

Bees have a narrow waist between their abdomen and thorax.

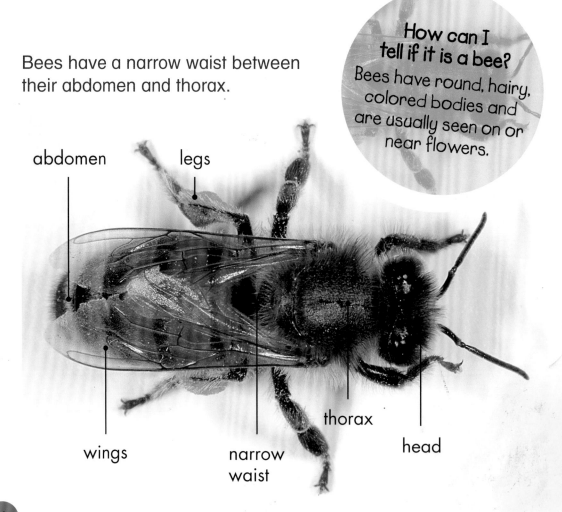

How can I tell if it is a bee? Bees have round, hairy, colored bodies and are usually seen on or near flowers.

abdomen

legs

wings

narrow waist

thorax

head

Most bees are very hairy. These hairs pick up **pollen** when bees visit flowers. Bees have a **proboscis** and **antennae** on their head.

A bee's proboscis is like a long straw that it uses to get food.

antennae for smelling

hairy legs and body for carrying pollen

proboscis for getting food

Different Types of Bees

There are more than 20,000 **species** of bees. About 500 species are **social** bees. The other species are **solitary** bees.

Honeybees are social bees that make and store honey in their hives.

Bumblebees are social bees that make a buzzing noise when they fly.

Blueberry bees are solitary bees that like to feed on blueberry flowers.

Some bees are yellow and black, but other species are red, green, or blue. The largest bees are almost 1½ inches (4 centimeters) long. The smallest are less than 1/12 inch (2 millimeters) long.

Leaf-cutter bees are some of the largest bees.

1½ inches (4 centimeters)

Some bee species are smaller than a pencil eraser!

1/12 inch (2 millimeters)

Where in the World Are Bees Found?

Bees are found almost everywhere in the world. The only areas where bees are not found are the Arctic and Antarctica.

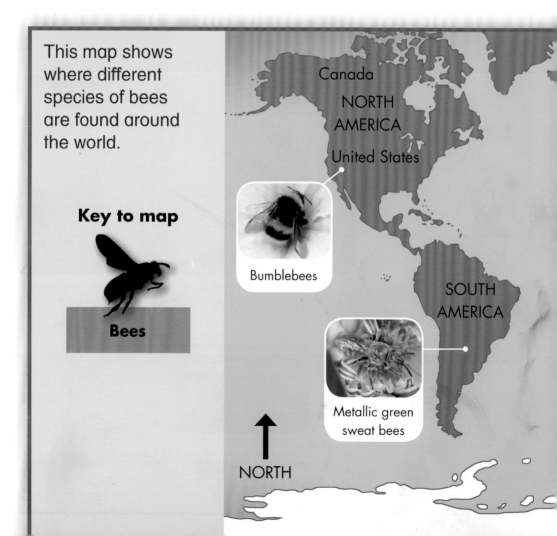

This map shows where different species of bees are found around the world.

Key to map

Bees

Canada

NORTH AMERICA

United States

Bumblebees

SOUTH AMERICA

Metallic green sweat bees

NORTH

Bees can be found in all places where there are flowers.

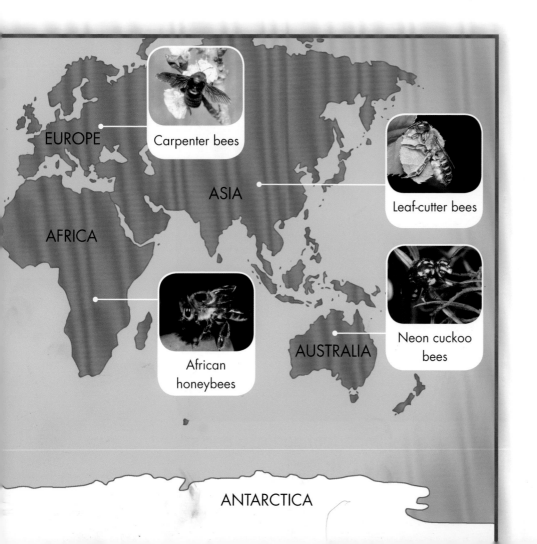

EUROPE

Carpenter bees

ASIA

Leaf-cutter bees

AFRICA

African honeybees

AUSTRALIA

Neon cuckoo bees

ANTARCTICA

Habitats of Bees

Bees live in **habitats** that have water, food, and shelter. These habitats include grasslands, forests with open spaces, and wetlands such as swamps. Bees also live in gardens and parks.

Flowers are the most important part of a bee's habitat because they provide food.

Many species of bees live in deserts. They survive the hot, dry weather by sleeping. This is called hibernation. After it rains, flowers grow and bees wake up to feed.

Some carpenter bees live in deserts, where they can feed on cactus flowers.

Life Cycles of Bees

A life cycle diagram shows the stages of a bee's life, from newborn to adult.

1. A male and a female bee **mate**. The female lays eggs in a nest and leaves food near the eggs.

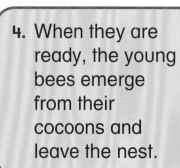

4. When they are ready, the young bees emerge from their cocoons and leave the nest.

Most bees live for only a few weeks.

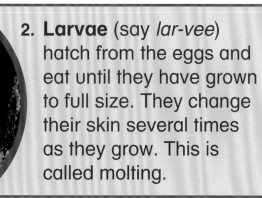

2. **Larvae** (say *lar-vee*) hatch from the eggs and eat until they have grown to full size. They change their skin several times as they grow. This is called molting.

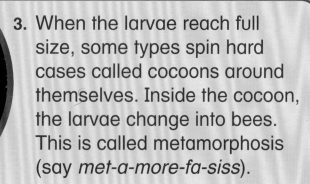

3. When the larvae reach full size, some types spin hard cases called cocoons around themselves. Inside the cocoon, the larvae change into bees. This is called metamorphosis (say *met-a-more-fa-siss*).

How Do Bees Live?

Most types of bees are solitary. Female bees spend their lives collecting food and making nests for their eggs. Male bees die soon after they mate.

This solitary leaf-cutter bee is carrying a leaf back to its nest.

Social bees live in large groups called colonies. Each colony has one queen bee and many worker bees that look after the larvae. Male bees are called drones.

Honeybees are social bees that make honey.

Bee Homes

Social bees live together in a home called a hive. Bees make their hives in holes in trees or between rocks. Some hives hang from tree branches.

Bee hives can be home to many thousands of bees.

Solitary bees do not live in a hive. When they need to rest, they can hang from a plant stem. Female bees can also sleep in their nest while they are making it.

Some solitary bees rest between the petals of a flower.

Bee Food

Bees eat **nectar** and pollen from flowers. Nectar is found inside flowers and pollen is found on the surface. Honeybees also eat honey.

Foods That Bees Eat

Flower nectar

Pollen

Honey

Bees use their proboscis to reach the nectar inside a flower. The hairs on their body pick up pollen. Some bees have special sacs on their legs to carry pollen.

A bee's proboscis is like a straw for sucking up flower nectar.

proboscis

sac

This bee is carrying pollen using sacs on its legs.

Why Do Bees Make Honey?

Some species of bees make honey as a way to store food. Honey is made from nectar. Some bees fly up to 6 miles (10 kilometers) to collect nectar before returning to their hive.

One bee can visit up to two thousand flowers in a day to collect nectar.

Back at the hive, the bees chew the nectar. They spread it on a waxy grid called a honeycomb. The nectar slowly gets thicker and becomes honey.

Bees store honey in their hives to feed themselves and their young.

Threats to the Survival of Bees

Bees are threatened by other animals. Many different **predators** feed on bees. These predators include:

- mammals, such as bears
- insects, such as ants and wasps
- birds, such as bee-eaters
- other bees
- spiders.

Lynx spiders jump on bees and eat them.

Tiny minibeasts called mites are a serious threat to honeybees. Mites hide on bees and are carried back to the hive, where they eat bee larvae.

These mites are hiding on the back of a honeybee.

mites

Stinging Bees

Most bees have stingers attached to the end of their abdomen. Bees use their stingers to protect their nest from attackers, such as other bees.

Only female bees have stingers.

stinger

Bees can use their stingers many times against other insects. However, if a bee stings a human, its stinger will stay in the skin. The bee will soon die.

When a bee stings a human, it leaves its stinger behind.

Bees and the Environment

Bees are an important part of the **environment** they live in. Bees feed on other animals and on plants, and many animals feed on them.
This is shown in a food web.

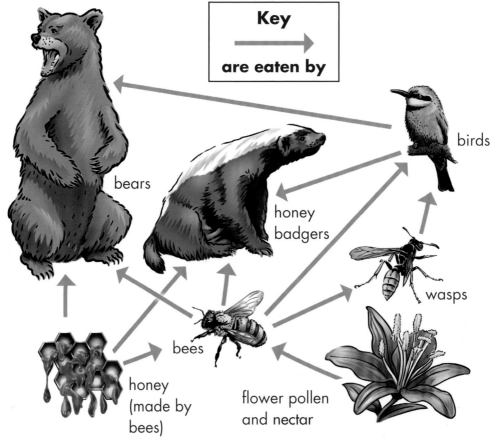

Key

are eaten by

bears

honey badgers

birds

wasps

bees

honey (made by bees)

flower pollen and nectar

This food web shows what bees eat and what eats them.

Flowers need to spread pollen to make new plants. This is called pollination. Bees help to pollinate plants that produce foods that humans eat, such as apples.

More than a quarter of the foods that people eat come from plants pollinated by bees.

Tips for Watching Bees

These tips will help you to watch bees:

- Look where there are flowers, because bees may be nearby.
- Put out some honey in a warm spot to attract any bees in the area.
- Listen for the buzzing sound that bees make.
- Avoid disturbing bees, because many bees sting.

Look but do not touch! Watch bees without touching them to see where they go and what they do.

Bees can be watched once they have landed on flowers.

Glossary

abdomen   The end section of an insect's body.

antennae   Organs found on the heads of insects, used for sensing things.

arachnids   Eight-legged animals, such as spiders, that are part of the arthropod group.

environment   The air, water, and land that surround us.

habitats   Areas in which animals are naturally found.

larvae   The young of an insect.

mate   Join together to produce young.

nectar   A sweet liquid made by flowers.

pollen   Yellow powder found on flowers.

predators   Animals that hunt other animals for food.

proboscis   A tube used for sucking up food.

social   Living with other animals in a group.

solitary   Living alone.

species   Groups of animals or plants that have similar features.

thorax   The part of the body between the head and abdomen.

Index